LETTERS
TO AN
ASPIRING
SCHOLAR

LETTERS
TO AN
ASPIRING
SCHOLAR

Embracing Creativity for Doctoral Scholarship &
Overcoming Obstacles in Everyday Life

Christopher M. Strickland

Copyright © 2022 Christopher M. Strickland
All rights reserved.

All artworks (collage, paintings, drawings, sketches, poetry and photography) by Christopher M. Strickland

Edited by Candi Dugas and Lyette Erin
Book and Cover Design by Lyette Erin
Cover Photograph by Christopher M. Strickland

ISBN: 978-1-942885-83-2

DEDICATION

With immense gratitude, I dedicate this book to:

Adaire Bane. For your presence in my life and willingness to be my muse.

Dr. Francine Jennings, Dr. Martha Barry McKenna, and Dr. Jane Dalton. For the indelible mark left on my heart from your mentorship and feedback throughout my doctoral journey.

Lesley University Educational Leadership Cohort '15. For all of your support, questions, and feedback, as well as accountability to our shared doctoral learning experience and one another.

TABLE OF CONTENTS

Table of Illustrations	xi
Acknowledgments	xiii
Preface	xv
Introduction	1
Letter 1: Connecting	7
Letter 2: To Know Thyself	17
Letter 3: Envisioning	27
Letter 4: Passion	37
Letter 5: Vulnerability	47
Letter 6: Boundaries	55
Letter 7: Discipline/Routines/Creative Practices	65
Letter 8: Writing	77
Letter 9: Reading	87
Letter 10: Cleaning and Organizing	95
Letter 11: Openness to Feedback	103
Letter 12: Waiting and Walking with Humility	111
Letter 13: Support Systems	121
Letter 14: Gratitude	129
Epilogue	139
References	145

TABLE OF ILLUSTRATIONS

FIGURE 1. "I AM FROM …" POEM.
© 2006 CHRISTOPHER M. STRICKLAND

FIGURE 2. "VISION BOARD"
© 2018 CHRISTOPHER M. STRICKLAND

FIGURE 3. "DOCTORAL JOURNEY TRIPTYCH"
© 2015–18 CHRISTOPHER M. STRICKLAND

ACKNOWLEDGMENTS

Writing this book has been cathartic for me. Throughout the course of my doctoral experience, I learned that academic writing is truly an art form, like my paintings. Understanding this parallel affirmed what I had known intuitively and grounded it within truth and experience. The ability to communicate in a variety of ways is priceless and necessary to connect with others. I am reminded of the words by Saint Francis of Assisi, "[Teach], and when necessary use words." The desire to write a book to serve others felt extremely purposeful in my soul. Intrinsically, this book is an extension of my creative teaching and learning practice. Through these pages I share first-hand experiences and acquired wisdom to help others become enlightened, and potentially transformed.

Letters to an Aspiring Scholar exists because of the critical help, support, and guidance of several individuals. First, my family and friends, who continue to support me in following my dreams and creative endeavors. Second, Candi Dugas, who graciously offered me invaluable editorial feedback at various stages of my projects. Third, members of the Lesley University Educational Leadership Doctoral Cohort '15, who have been supportive every step of the way, engaging me with great questions and fascinating dialogue. We have learned so much from each other, and I hope this book provides a completely satisfying response to all their queries. Finally, Lyette Erin, for her interest and publication vision, and Patricia Oman and the Hastings College Press for their support.

PREFACE

I was inspired to write this book for two reasons: To answer probing questions from others regarding how I completed my dissertation so efficiently and to respond to the challenge of a thought-provoking TED Talk about dignity and serving the public good.

Writing this book allowed me to reflect deeply upon my journey of earning a doctorate degree and to explore various forms of creative expression and personal meaning-making. Furthermore, the idea of sharing the wisdom gleaned from my doctoral experience resonated with my personal desire to help others and act with purpose.

My completion of a dissertation and a doctorate began as a lofty dream that was deconstructed into various doable steps. The first step was to set a goal. My goal was to engage doctoral study and complete my dissertation within three years. Because I was able to make and take doable steps, I ended up completing my doctoral program in less than three years, as my research and dissertation took only eight months, which I understand is an impressive feat and a record for Lesley University's PhD program in Educational Studies and Educational Leadership Specialization.

As a result, my colleagues and cohort members have been asking, "How did you do it?" They have also been requesting my guidance: "Please give me your secrets to bring this journey to a merciful and speedy conclusion." I have spent some time reflecting on these queries and thinking about how to articulate steps for what has been mostly an intuitive process for me.

An important step to note is my resignation from a 16-year career of teaching public school at the start of the third year of my doctoral program. Becoming a full-time doctoral student allowed me to focus on my research and complete my dissertation relatively quickly. Despite that opportunity of full-time focus, my success depended on more than just having the time, though. It really was about time management and how I approached the doctoral work, using various methods of self-discipline along with creativity to engage doctoral scholarship.

Around the same time of contemplating how I disciplined myself using creative processes, I watched a TED Talk by John Cary, an architect and designer. Cary spoke about the importance of creating architecture and designing with dignity for the public good. He believed design has the unique ability to dignify people and make them feel valued, respected, honored, and seen. Through a personal story, Cary pointed out that architects and designers tend to be disconnected from the people they are serving, creating spaces that do not consider their uniqueness or their needs. Subsequently, Cary called for architects and designers to consider diversity, uniqueness, and serving the public good rather than a privileged few.

John Cary's message about dignity and serving the public good deeply resonates with me. As I have been thinking about how to respond to the questions posed by my colleagues and cohort members, the concepts of connection and serving others have been lingering in my mind. Because I am an artist educator and autoethnographic researcher, the idea to design and create a book using personal experiences to examine and explore a cultural understanding and appreciation for doctoral study seemed apropos. As John Cary eloquently states, "The spaces you inhabit reflect back your value."

This book is my reflection, my authentic response to connect with others and create a space that specifically serves the needs of individuals who are thinking about pursuing doctoral study and/or are already engaging in their research and struggling with writing their dissertation. Likewise, this book also serves a significant and universal purpose for those who desire to overcome obstacles that prevent them from living the life they have imagined.

INTRODUCTION

TEA WITH ADAIRE

Recently, I enjoyed tea with a former student of mine, Adaire. Adaire is graduating soon with her bachelor's degree from Lesley University. She and I have a unique relationship; I have known her, literally since the beginning of my teaching career. We have "grown up" together. I first met Adaire when she was in elementary school; I was her art teacher. We lost touch when she moved on to middle school, and then we reconnected when she matriculated high school. By that time, I had transitioned from teaching elementary art to teaching secondary art, and Adaire was a student in several of my art classes in high school. Then, once again, as a young adult, she became a student of mine during her junior year in college when I began a teaching assistant position at Lesley as a doctoral candidate.

During our recent tea session, Adaire reminded me of our intertwined history, and we both chuckled as she commented, "It feels like you have been following me." Adaire then told me that I inspire her and that she plans to pursue her graduate education, including a doctorate degree. This news warmed my heart because I know we share the same proclivity for creativity, community, and scholarship. I began to think about how fortunate I am to have had the opportunity to witness her growth and to learn from her as well throughout all these years. It has been an honor for me as well to be an influence in the life of this remarkable person.

I shared with Adaire my idea for writing a book about how I successfully engaged doctoral study and how I completed my dissertation in less than three years. She indicated that she would appreciate a resource like that. As we were discussing the possibilities of this book, an idea blossomed in my head. While I had been thinking about the content, I was still somewhat uncertain of the book's organization and layout. My interactions with Adaire over the years began to remind me of the book, *Letters to a Young Poet*, by Rainer Maria Rilke. Instantly with a jolt, I was inspired!

With fascination, I described to Adaire how fittingly creative I think my book would be if I were to write it in the manner of Rilke, as if I were writing letters to an intended individual. It was in that moment I decided to use Adaire as my muse, to write to her, sharing my wisdom. She would become a composite character, symbolizing the relationships I have had with students and members of my doctoral program's cohort.

Thus, I entitle this book, *Letters to an Aspiring Scholar*. Along with writing it in the tradition of Rilke, it nods to others such as Julia Cameron and Jonathan Kozol, who have found value using the literary device of writing warm, friendly letters, in effort to support those in need of encouragement, wisdom, and strategies for success in their endeavors.

AN OVERVIEW OF THE BOOK

This book is rooted in the academic methodology of autoethnography. According to Adams, Holman Jones, and Ellis (2015), "autoethnographic stories: are stories of/about the self—told through the lens of culture. Autoethnographic stories are artistic and analytic demonstrations of how we come to know, name, and interpret personal and cultural experience." This book has fourteen letters (chapters), not including this introduction.

I use the form of letters to enhance the book's offering of encouragement, guidance, and strategies for doctoral students in all phases of their doctoral study, but especially with writing the dissertation.

The letters are sequenced to represent the methodical way I engaged the dissertation phase of my doctoral program. Letters one to six discuss the dispositions and characteristics that I cultivated to embrace creatively doctoral work. Letters seven to ten contextualize and focus on the routines and creative practices I used to discipline myself for doctoral study and writing my dissertation. I describe specific strategies and action steps in detail and provide supplemental resources at the end of each letter. Letters eleven to fourteen highlight specific insights I gained from engaging the entire doctoral experience and how these understandings holistically provide wisdom for the greater journey of life.

I desire that the wisdom I offer serves to help readers understand the dispositions, routines, and creative practices that I used to help me succeed in writing my dissertation and completing my doctoral program in less than three years. If you are a doctoral candidate, I hope this book is useful for helping you achieve your goal to complete your dissertation and doctoral program successfully. Perhaps more importantly, I hope the strategies shared within these letters are inspiring and become beneficial processes that can help anyone overcome any obstacles in life that prevent them from living the way they have imagined.

1
CONNECTING

As unique as we all are, an awful lot of us want the same things. We want to shake up our current less-than fulfilling lives.

We want to be happier, more loving, forgiving and connected with the people around us.
—Brené Brown

The key to the happy life, it seems, is the good life: a life with sustained relationships, challenging work, and connections to community.
—Paul Bloom

Creativity is just connecting things. When you ask creative people how they did something, they feel a little guilty because they didn't really do it, they just saw something. It seemed obvious to them after a while. That's because they were able to connect experiences they've had and synthesize new things.
—Steve Jobs

April 13, 2018

Dear Adaire,

 I am so grateful that you have reached out to me. Your inquiry about doctoral study and the process of completing a dissertation is auspicious. I can sense the curiosity in your words when you ask, "How did you do it?" How I completed and successfully defended my dissertation to earn a doctorate degree in less than three years does seem to be the "Million Dollar" question. It is my pleasure to share with you my wisdom, tips, strategies, and experiences of doctoral scholarship.

 I am sure you can imagine the magnitude of the journey you are about to begin. Did you know that, according to the United States Census Bureau data from the 2016 American Census Survey, only 2% of the American population has a doctorate degree? This percentage of individuals in the United States is very small.

 As a result, within our culture, there are many interesting assumptions, mythologies, and flawed perceptions surrounding academia and doctoral scholarship. Given this challenge, I will do my best to share with you my experiences and the reality I have come to know from engaging in doctoral scholarship. I hope that my "pearls of wisdom" will not only inspire you but prove helpful for your own doctoral journey.

 I encourage you to try all the activities I present to you. I must warn, though, that I cannot guarantee these tools will work the same for you as they did for me. However, I think they cannot hurt, and they are worth a try! After all, knowing is personal and the result of how you synthesize information, ideas, and concepts for your own meaning-making.

 My first instinct is to share others' words of wisdom that have been a source of inspiration to me. As you know, I have always found comfort in a good quote; so, I thought I would begin each letter to you by sharing some of the quotes that not only inspire me but also capture the essence of the themes within each letter that I write you. I hope you will find the quotes as meaningful as I do.

 In addition to the inspiring quotes, I am also going to share some visual expressions with you. As an artist educator, my creative learning process involves visually expressing concepts for sense-making. So, sketches and drawings accompany each letter. These images are reflective expressions that visually emphasize the message I wish to convey. To this end, I believe the information I share with you will be both illuminating and instructive.

I am very excited about this opportunity to connect with you; it will be beneficial for me as well. Reflecting upon my doctoral journey and the road to completing my dissertation will be a cathartic experience. Thank you for contacting me and please do not hesitate to ask any questions along the way!

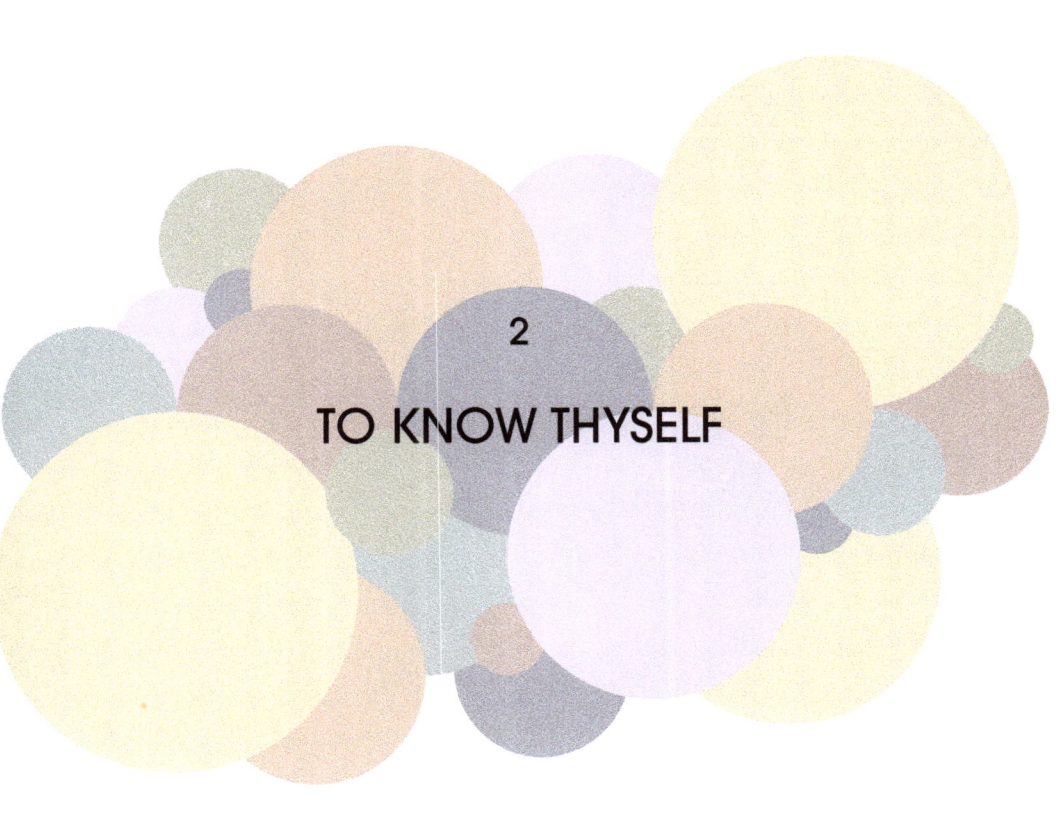

2
TO KNOW THYSELF

"I Am," the two most powerful words in the English language.
—Deborah Willis

To engage the known with one's whole self ... to know in truth is to be known as well.
—Parker Palmer

Know from whence you came. If you know whence you came, there are absolutely no limitations to where you can go.
—James Baldwin

April 16, 2018

Dear Adaire,

I have been thinking about where to begin during these last few days. Without wanting to sound too cliché, I believe it is important that we start at the beginning. In this context, the beginning is you—literally.

Who are you?

Your immediate response will most likely begin with the words, "I am." I think it is important that you take some time to reflect upon the potency of these two words. Explore your sense of self and identity.

I'm sure you're wondering why I am having you think about identity, and what identity and the words "I am" have to do with doctoral scholarship or the creation of your dissertation. The words "I am" are ancient and deeply associated with Judeo-Christian religious meaning. However, within the context of doctoral scholarship, I am interested in looking at these words in relation to examining or knowing oneself.

When you begin doctoral work, it is important that you know yourself.

Knowing who you are serves several purposes. First, you can own your identity. Second, you begin to see how your sense of self connects with others and the world around you. Third, you can then articulate a sense of self and communicate this to others.

Identities are mostly derived from our social and cultural experiences. These experiences shape our consciousness and affect the context in which knowledge is constructed. Therefore, your social and cultural experiences will inevitably influence how you approach doctoral research, such as formulating your guiding research questions or deciding what research design and methodology is appropriate for your dissertation scholarship.

During the first residency of my doctoral program, all the candidates were gathered in the university amphitheater, and the director of the PhD program challenged us "To Know Thyself." Particularly, he noted that doctoral students who are interested in qualitative research must reflect upon their sociocultural perspective, the significant social and cultural factors that have influenced their lives, work, and scholarship.

What this means is that individuals must examine where they have been and how they think, and learn how this understanding impacts their sense of bias and connection to the research work on which they are focusing. Understanding the concept of sociocultural perspective is essential.

This understanding is so important because during the dissertation phase, the doctoral candidate must demonstrate a heightened awareness of how their individual identity and the epistemological and philosophical orientations of the research approach affect how the inquiry is conducted and the knowledge generated by the inquiry.

James Baldwin wrote, "Know from whence you came. If you know whence you came, there are absolutely no limitations to where you can go." These words hold a very valuable truth, especially for doctoral candidates embarking on their research and dissertations. Qualitative research is exploratory, and its researchers aim to discover and understand the lived experiences of others.

In order for qualitative researchers to be successful in understanding others, they must have first-hand experience and a clear understanding of themselves. Another way to think about this concept is by equating it to RuPaul's iconic mantra, "If you can't love yourself, how the hell are you gonna love somebody else?"

My first bit of advice is that before you move forward, look back and reflect. To know thyself is key to engaging your doctoral research and dissertation. Examining one's sociocultural perspective is a reflective journey into self-discovery.

One of the ways I began my own journey of self-discovery was through writing an "I Am From ..." poem (Figure 1). I present this example to you as a strategy and means to recognize how I approached self-reflection through creativity, for me to "know thyself" and to make sense of the concept of sociocultural perspective.

As you begin your doctoral journey, I think you should allow yourself to be creative and write a poem about who you are and where you are from. Once this frame of understanding is internally espoused in your mind and heart, it will influence your epistemological and philosophical perspectives, assumptions, and approaches for conducting research.

To help you, I have included the following action steps or directions to engage this creative activity. If you decide to try this creative activity and write an "I Am From ..." poem, please consider sharing your work with me. You know how much I love poetry, and it would also be an honor to read yours.

I Am From

I am from a place of experience …
where things are complex and not as simple,
except for when they are

A place where artistry and scholarship are one and the same,
as creative exploration is desired and making mistakes is required

A place where love in all its mystery
eludes as to not be defined, confined or categorized

A place where prayers are selfless
and miracles are acts of love waiting to set us free

A place where truth and integrity are precious,
valued far more than any finite possessions

A place where being normal is not a virtue
and diversity is celebrated and revered

A place where letting go is not the same as losing control—
after all, you cannot lose what you never had

I am from a realm of endless possibilities …
knowing that what I am today is not all that I will be tommorrow

FIGURE 1. "I AM FROM…" POEM © 2006 CMS

Creative Activity: "I Am From ..." Poem

MATERIALS

- ☐ Paper (lined or unlined—whatever your preference)
- ☐ Writing utensil(s) (pens or pencils)
- ☐ Computer and/or word processing software

ACTION STEPS

1. Take the time to reflect and think about your memories, past, and upbringing. Focus on the details of events or experiences, your life, and memories (and the feelings associated with them).
2. Insert the phrase "I am from ..." as often as you would like to organize and emphasize the personal nature of your thoughts, feelings, and experiences.
3. The poem is considered free verse, which means there is no specific structure and it does not need to rhyme, but it can if you want it to!
4. The poem is as long as it needs to be to convey the message and insights you discover.
5. Hang or place a completed copy of your "I Am From ..." poem by your work space for routine viewing and affirmation.

RESOURCES

Collom, J. & Noethe, S. (Eds.). (2005). *Poetry everywhere*. New York, NY: T&W Books.

Padget, R. (Ed.). (2000). *Handbook of poetic forms*. New York, NY: T&W Books.

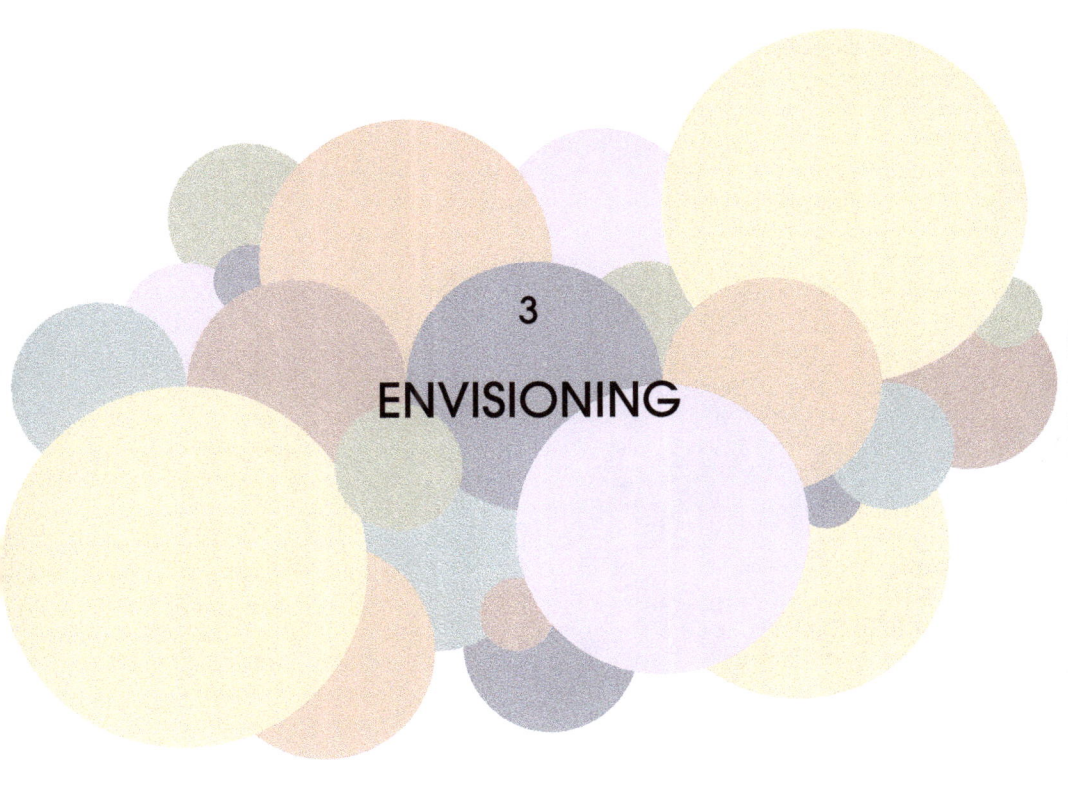

3
ENVISIONING

If you can dream it, you can do it.

—Walt Disney

Logic will get you from A to B. Imagination will take you everywhere.

—Albert Einstein

Intention is power. Intention is ownership. Intention is commitment.

—Sonia Choquette

April 18, 2018

Dear Adaire,

    I am pleased to hear that you have taken my advice and allowed yourself the opportunity to create an "I Am From …" poem. Poetry, like all artistic forms, is a powerful way of knowing, communicating, and expressing the depths of the human heart and mind. You will find that many of the strategies or activities I present to you involve the arts, creativity, and aesthetic experiences to foster discipline and create an engaging and learning-centered environment for your doctoral work.

    After all, as I am an artist educator, would you expect anything less? Another tool I use to help focus my attention and direction for many things in my life, including my doctoral study, is the creation of a vision board. Have you heard of or ever created a vision board before? The process is rooted in the visual arts, specifically the technique of collage. Collaging is the process of assembling different materials—like photographs, pieces of paper, or fabric—to make a new whole.

    The experience of creating a vision board engages your imagination and capacity for mindfulness, as you intentionally combine various images, text, and relevant materials that reflect your interests, desires, and goals. You assemble all of the materials and secure them onto a piece of paper or poster board to display in an ideal location, a place where you will see it every day. For example, I hang my vision boards over my desk. When I sit down to work, I notice it, reminding me of my goals and dreams. In Figure 2 you can see my vision board as an example for you.

    Creating a vision board uses your imagination and intentions to visualize and hone in on your ideas. The reinforcement of seeing the imagery of your vision board, whether it is pictures or text, becomes a daily form of motivation and reminder of what you want to achieve. The more you focus your attention to the information presented in the vision board, the greater clarity and ideas are generated to actualize your desire in order to make it a reality.

    The act of creating anything artistic is powerful and the expression becomes a metaphor for action, as well as achievement. I strongly encourage you to engage this visual art activity. Make a vision board of how you envision and what you desire from your doctoral journey. However, do not be too serious about it. Simply have fun imagining, envisioning, and creating your vision board! When you do, will you please consider taking a picture and sharing it with me? Not only am I curious about what you will create, but talking about your vision board and intentions behind it also allows your vision and goal to become actualized, especially when you share it with those who support and believe in you. I offer the following action steps and directions to help you begin the vision board activity.

Creative Activity: Vision Board

MATERIALS

- ☐ Paper or poster board
    - » Size is always a preference, but in this case, the bigger the vision/dream, the larger the size paper you would want to use to manifest your envisioning!
- ☐ Scissors
- ☐ Glue or Modge Podge®
- ☐ Magazines and newspapers
    - » Choose publications with content relevant to the purpose of your board. For a doctoral journey, choose those with education, higher education, and/or content-specific information.
- ☐ Photographs, printed images, drawing paper, markers, colored pencils, paint, fabric
- ☐ Computer with a printer and internet access

ACTION STEPS

1. Sit down and set an intention for the purpose of your vision board.
    - » Explore and collect imagery, text, and items that represent your intentions. What do you want to do with your doctorate degree? How do you foresee using it?
2. Take the time to arrange and collage the materials into an aesthetically pleasing composition. Then secure the materials using the glue or Modge Podge®.

3. Once the vision board is dried, hang it in a prominent place where you will see it daily and be inspired.
4. Remember that the vision board is a metaphor for action. Reflect often about what it is you desire and how you can take steps to achieve your goal.

RESOURCES

Assarraf, J. (2008). *The complete vision board kit: Using the power of intention and visualization to achieve your dreams.* Hillsboro, OR: Beyond Words Publishing.

Choquette, S. (2016). *Your 3 best super powers: Meditation, imagination and intuition.* Carlsbad, CA: Hay House, Inc.

FIGURE 2. "VISION BOARD" © 2018 CMS

4
PASSION

Passion is energy. Feel the power that comes from focusing on what excites you.

—Oprah Winfrey

Never underestimate the vital importance of finding early in life the work that for you is play. This turns possible underachievers into happy warriors.

—Sir Ken Robinson

April 22, 2018

Dear Adaire,

 What are you passionate about? What is the value of doctoral work to you? In this letter, I want to talk about the critical connection between passion and doctoral study. By discovering your passion, you will perceive what Sir Ken Robinson referred to as "the element" and realize how finding your passion changes everything, which is especially true when you integrate your passion into the doctoral work you are pursuing. There are two types of passion I want you to consider.

 First, as a doctoral candidate, you must be passionate about what you're studying. During the second year of my doctoral program, one of my professors told me that you must have a passion for what you choose to do for research and the dissertation. This fervor is so important because you will be working on your research and dissertation for an extensive amount of time. Equally important to having a certain zeal for your research topic are the practices you use to sustain your interest during the arduous process of doctoral study. I have found many practices to be quite effective for stimulating my senses and engaging my heart and mind during my dissertation phase.

 For example, employing simple rituals such as lighting scented candles while reading literature or listening to music that is inspiring while writing your dissertation will help to fuel your passion. Integrating simple rituals with your doctoral scholarship brings validation and excitement to the work you are doing. It makes the moments purposeful as it fills your senses with desire. You will find that invoking simple rituals can also propel you out of momentary funks, moving you forward to achieving your goal of completing your dissertation.

 Second, as a sentient being who is wired for creativity, you must engage and express your passion through creativity. It is vital to balance your doctoral study with passionate play, as well as the pursuit of your creative interests. Figure 3 is one example of some artwork I created to document my entire doctoral experience and learning process.

 The three abstract watercolor paintings together form a triptych that symbolize each year of my doctoral journey. Interestingly, painting has allowed me to process ideas and understand the doctoral work I engaged in from a different perspective and language.

 As mentioned previously, my creative learning process involves drawing, doodling, and making art for sense-making. For example, it was not uncommon for me to work in tandem on a painting and a chapter of my dissertation. I have always engaged painting to experience the joy, wonder, and power of creating and reflecting. This creatively diverse engagement is a significant part of what inspires me as an educator of art. You have told me that dance is your artistic medium of preference. I recommend that you dance through some of your thinking and processing. I think you will be surprised at the clarity and balance that comes from integrating your passion and scholarship.

Balancing doctoral study and dissertation writing with any creative outlet is important. I want to emphasize that creativity does not necessarily mean engaging in the arts. There are different ways to be creative besides engaging in the arts. I only focused on artistic examples because you and I understand and are passionate about the arts.

Essentially, engaging in whatever you are passionate about will serve you well. In order not to get sick of your topic of study, or if you are easily distracted and your enthusiasm starts to fade, consider reminding yourself of the purpose of your doctoral study by engaging your element or passion and through simple rituals that stimulate your senses. I provide the following list of resources to help you explore your passion in relation to doctoral study. These resources are some that I have found to be extremely helpful during the process of completing any of my projects, including my doctoral study.

RESOURCES

Literature

Csikszentmihalyi, M. (1996/2013). *Creativity: The psychology of discovery and invention.* New York, NY: HarperCollins Publishers.

Greene, M. (1995). *Releasing the imagination.* San Francisco, CA: Jossey-Bass.

Robinson, K. (2009). *The element.* New York, NY: The Penguin Group.

Robinson, K. (2013). *Finding your element.* New York, NY: The Penguin Group.

Video

Wagner, T. (2009, April). Play, passion, purpose. [Video file]. Retrieved from *https://www.youtube.com/watch?v=hvDjh4l-VHo*

Music

SonicAid™

The Hillard Ensemble™

Any classical/instrumental, new age, or environmental soundscapes recording.

SCENTED CANDLES

Yankee Candles™ or Way Out Wax—Green Mountain Collection™

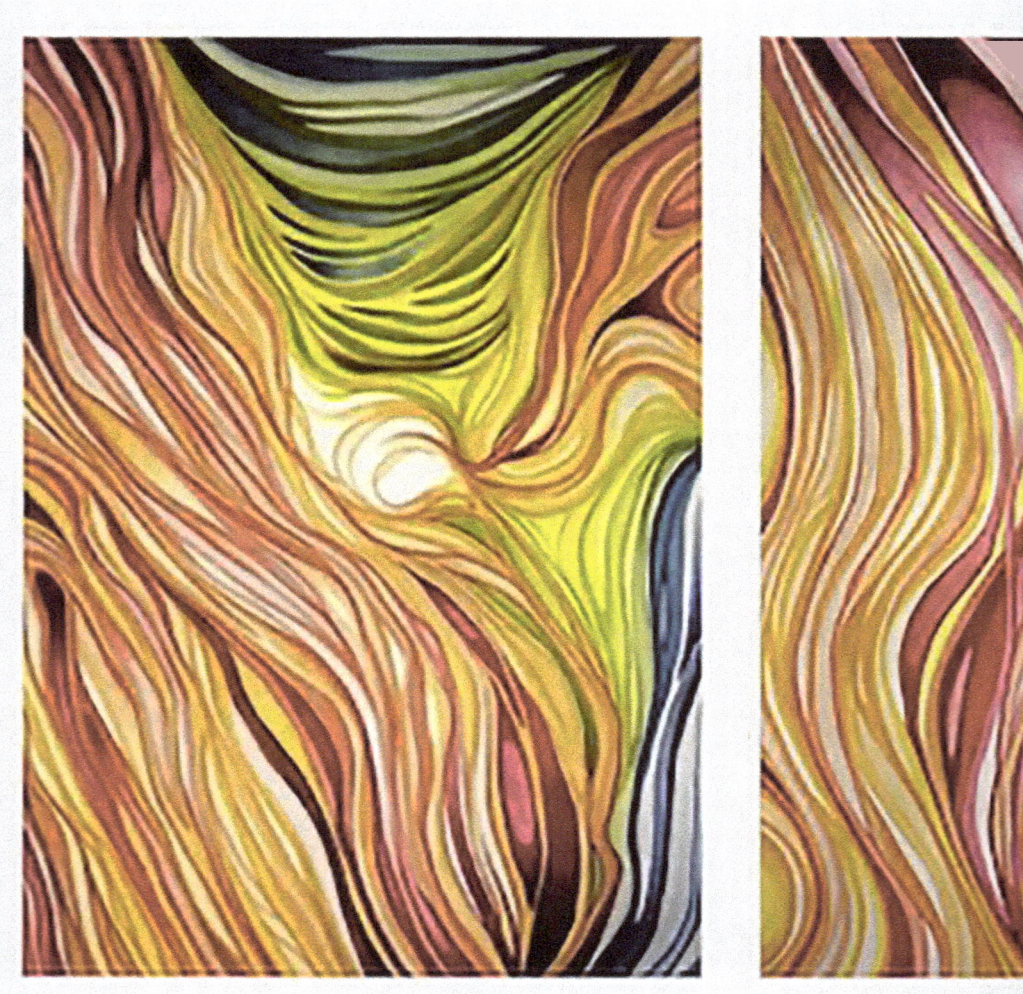

FIGURE 3. DOCTORAL JOURNEY TRIPTYCH © 2015–18 CMS

5
VULNERABILITY

Vulnerability is not weakness. Vulnerability is our most accurate measurement of courage—to be vulnerable, to let ourselves be seen, to be honest.

—Brené Brown

Knowing requires a personal relation between the knower and the known …

—Parker Palmer

April 28, 2018

Dear Adaire,

I am so happy that you made a vision board and I appreciate the digital photo you sent. Your vision board is fascinating. I am learning a lot about you, as the images in your vision board discloses so much about you as a person and student. This awareness has reminded me of the power of vulnerability and inspires this letter.

Education is a relational practice of entering community with others to share, learn, and grow. We know this concept as the "to know as we are known" approach, coined by Parker Palmer (1993). The essence of Palmer's belief is that the best way to have transformative experiences is to know ourselves, accept ourselves, and share ourselves. To engage others in an authentic manner such as this requires individuals to embrace vulnerability.

Many myths surround vulnerability, and the most notorious one is that vulnerability is a weakness. To address this inaccuracy and to counter the prevalent myths surrounding the concept of vulnerability, researcher Brené Brown defined vulnerability as "emotional risk, exposure, uncertainty" and noted that it is also the "birthplace of innovation, creativity, and change." In a culture of competitiveness and self-absorption, being authentic or vulnerable can be very difficult.

Despite the challenge, I cannot overemphasize the importance of embracing the power of vulnerability. Nobody ever said doctoral scholarship was easy. Inevitably, individuals who embark on this type of journey will struggle. Even I had my moments. Examples of my struggles include discovering my academic voice and learning to write with clarity and conciseness. I also wrestled with the uncertainty of research and scholarship results, trusting the process, protecting research participants, and the very act of creating a dissertation. These challenges were all real experiences that required me to embrace vulnerability in order to work through the grind of the doctoral process. This embrace was especially important to understand because vulnerability is inextricably linked to creativity.

According to Brené Brown, "creativity, which is the expression of our originality, helps us stay mindful that what we bring to the world is completely original and cannot be compared." Would you agree that writing a dissertation is a contribution to the world and an expression of an individual's creativity?

As a doctoral candidate and burgeoning qualitative researcher-scholar, you will need to open yourself to brand new experiences and engage a practice that involves working with people.

Scholarship, like other forms of work, becomes more meaningful when you authentically engage and connect with others. One of the ways you can begin to embrace vulnerability in doctoral study is by establishing a strong connection with your doctoral senior advisor. Such a connection means that you will be transparent with communicating your feelings and thoughts regarding the doctoral process and the experiences you are having. Your senior advisor is a mentor and confidant through your doctoral process. Your advisor can only support you to the extent to which you are willing to own and embrace your vulnerability, as you engage doctoral scholarship.

In order to do this, have the courage to face your fears by asking questions and opening yourself to the discomfort of the process that is intended to expand your perspective. When you do embrace vulnerability you will discover, as Brené Brown has exclaimed, that "vulnerability is the birthplace of innovation, creativity and change." Subsequently, the power of vulnerability can profoundly affect the way you live, work, and engage scholarship.

I would be remiss if I did not point out that our exchanges through these letters is another example of embracing vulnerability and being authentic. We are deepening further our relationship and building a community in which we can both share our hearts and thoughts, in an effort to experience our own personal transformation. How wonderful and inspiring to cultivate the wisdom each of us possesses and to share and benefit one another!

Thank you for letting me be courageous and share my vulnerability through these exchanges. I also thank you for finding a safe space with me in which you may be vulnerable. The following is a list of some resources that examine further the concepts of community, relationships, creativity, and vulnerability. Brené Brown and Parker Palmer are two of my heroes, and I highly recommend that you check out their respective bodies of work.

RESOURCES

Brown, B. (2010). *The gifts of imperfection.* Center City, MN: Hazelden.

Brown, B. (2012). *The power of vulnerability: Teachings on authenticity, connection, and courage.* [CD]. Boulder, CO: Sounds True.

Brown, B. (2012). *Daring greatly: How the courage to be vulnerable transforms the way we live, love, parent and lead.* New York, NY: Gotham Books.

Palmer, P. (1983/1993). *To know as we are known: Education as a spiritual practice.* New York, NY: HarperOne.

Palmer, P. (1997/2007). *The courage to teach.* San Francisco, CA: Jossey-Bass.

6
BOUNDARIES

How can we expect people to put value on our work when we don't value ourselves enough to set and hold uncomfortable boundaries?
—Brené Brown

Boundary setting is really a huge part of time management.
—Jim Loehr

Only you know what you can and want to give, and only you can be responsible for drawing that line. If you do not draw it, you can quickly become resentful.
—Dr. Henry Cloud & Dr. John Townsend

April 30, 2018

Dear Adaire,

    Building on the premise of my last letter regarding vulnerability, I want to note the significance of boundaries. Boundaries are essential to vulnerability and authenticity because they are "a function of self-respect and self-love" (Brown, 2015). One of the most difficult things you will have to do is to create boundaries that allow you to manage your time for doctoral work.

    Within this context, boundaries reflect a clear articulation of what your needs are, as well as the behaviors and actions that are acceptable and unacceptable for you as you engage your doctoral study. Setting boundaries can be a difficult process for anyone to do, especially when it involves family, friends, colleagues, and work.

    However, you must establish boundaries to help yourself and others respect and appreciate your time management and commitment to your doctoral study. The good news is that boundaries are flexible and can adjust as needed. Take comfort in knowing that doctoral study and writing your dissertation are a temporary process, and as the old adage states, "this too shall pass." Identifying and communicating your boundaries to those around you will help to make it easier for you stay focused and inspired to finish what you have started.

    Getting others to recognize and respect your boundaries is challenging, but not impossible. It will require some work on your part to stand firm and clear about what boundaries you are setting and why you are setting them. Taking the time to communicate as often as needed is important, because this will most likely be a new experience for you and those close to you. Although there is some discomfort in setting and holding boundaries, it will ultimately serve your integrity. Having integrity and engaging authentically creates stronger connection with others and will alleviate any resentment or disappointment you might feel if your needs are not respected or honored.

    Boundaries can take many forms. Within the context of my doctoral work, I established the following boundaries. First, I had to speak to my family and friends to tell them that doctoral study required a lot of solitary time to think and work. This demand on my time would mean that I could become withdrawn and miss certain events, functions, or social gatherings. For example, instead of attending weekly family dinners each month, I could possibly attend only one. It was important that I clearly communicated to my loved ones that my absence from certain gatherings or situations was not a reflection on them, but on my need to take the time to do the doctoral work. Second, I planned, organized, and informed others of my work schedule. For example, I let people know that during a certain timeframe of the day I would not be available to talk, text, or email, due to concentrating on reading, writing, or thinking. Third, I needed to limit external distractions, so I stopped engaging in social media, like Facebook, Twitter, Snapchat, or Instagram. Fourth, I not only scheduled time to work but also scheduled time to balance work with my creative outlets and social dates to connect with people as best I could. This schedule helped to organize and structure my time, and allowed me to engage with others in a special way, something that could be anticipated and about which to become excited. Since doctoral work requires so much time to reflect and process, do not be surprised that those who have not experienced doctoral work may struggle with the boundaries you establish. (Remember, pursuing and achieving a doctorate puts us in a small percentage of the population.) In the beginning of your doctoral journey, it is not uncommon for others to accuse you of disappearing or acting selfish with your time or to dislike your ability to respectfully decline invitations or to say "no" to things that would distract you from focusing on your doctoral study.

The best thing you can do is to communicate clearly, respectfully, and lovingly about setting the boundaries that you need to focus and complete your doctoral work. If you are not aware of or are not used to setting boundaries, you will most likely feel guilty for creating them. This feeling and experience is normal. Trust yourself and your intuition to do what is necessary for you to achieve the goal of earning your doctorate. Stand firmly in honoring your needs, and honor others by communicating your boundaries as well as you can.

Holding yourself and others accountable to respecting your boundaries will allow you to maintain integrity, engage authentically, and ultimately strengthen your relationships and connections with others. I leave you with the following resources that explore the concept of boundaries; I think you might find them helpful.

RESOURCES

Brown, B. (2015). *Rising strong: The reckoning, the rumble, the revolution.* New York, NY: Spiegel & Grau.

Brown, B. (2017). *Braving the wilderness: The quest for true belonging and the courage to stand alone.* New York, NY: Random House.

Cloud, H. & Townsend, J. (1992/2017). *Boundaries.* Grand Rapids, MI: Zondervan.

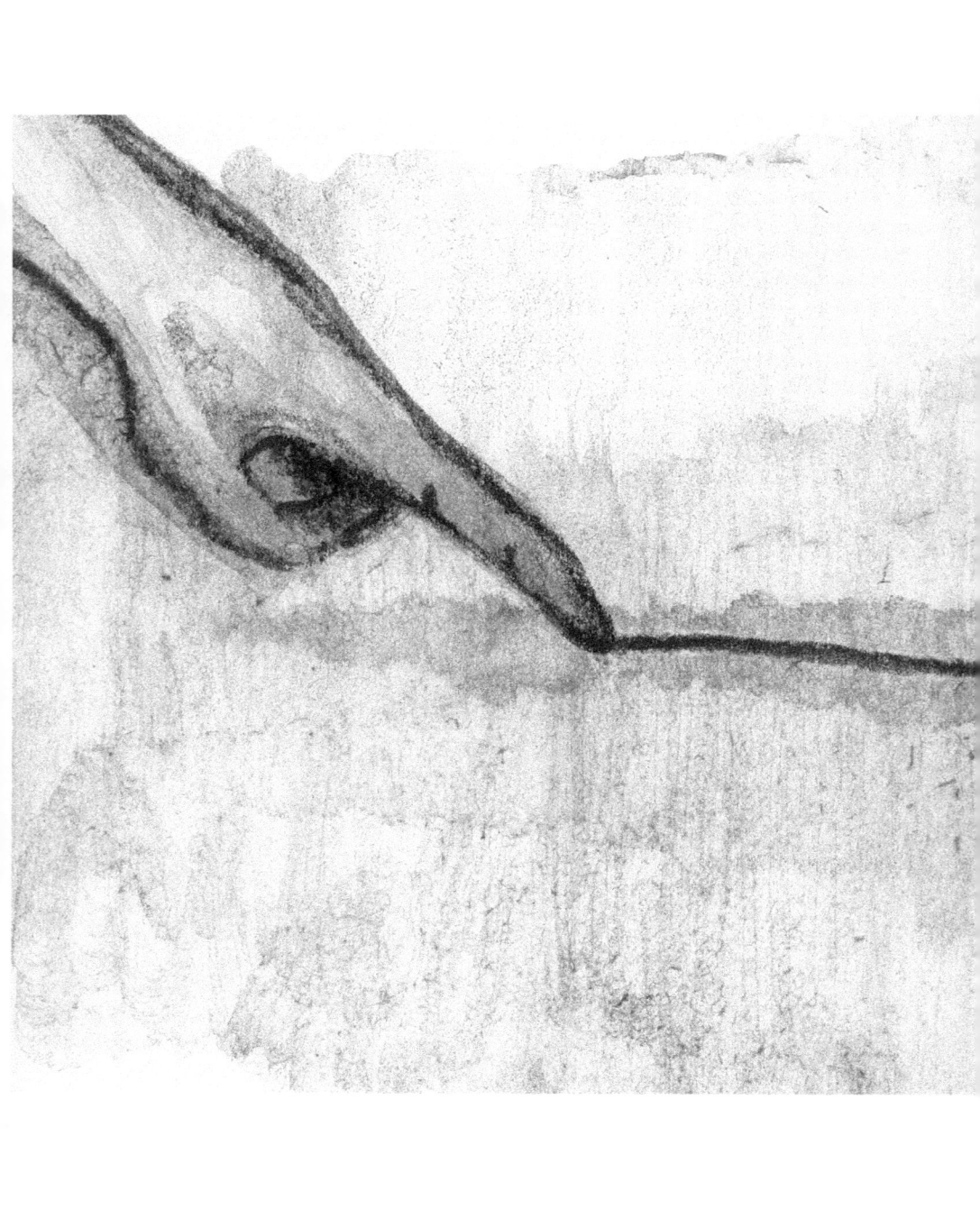

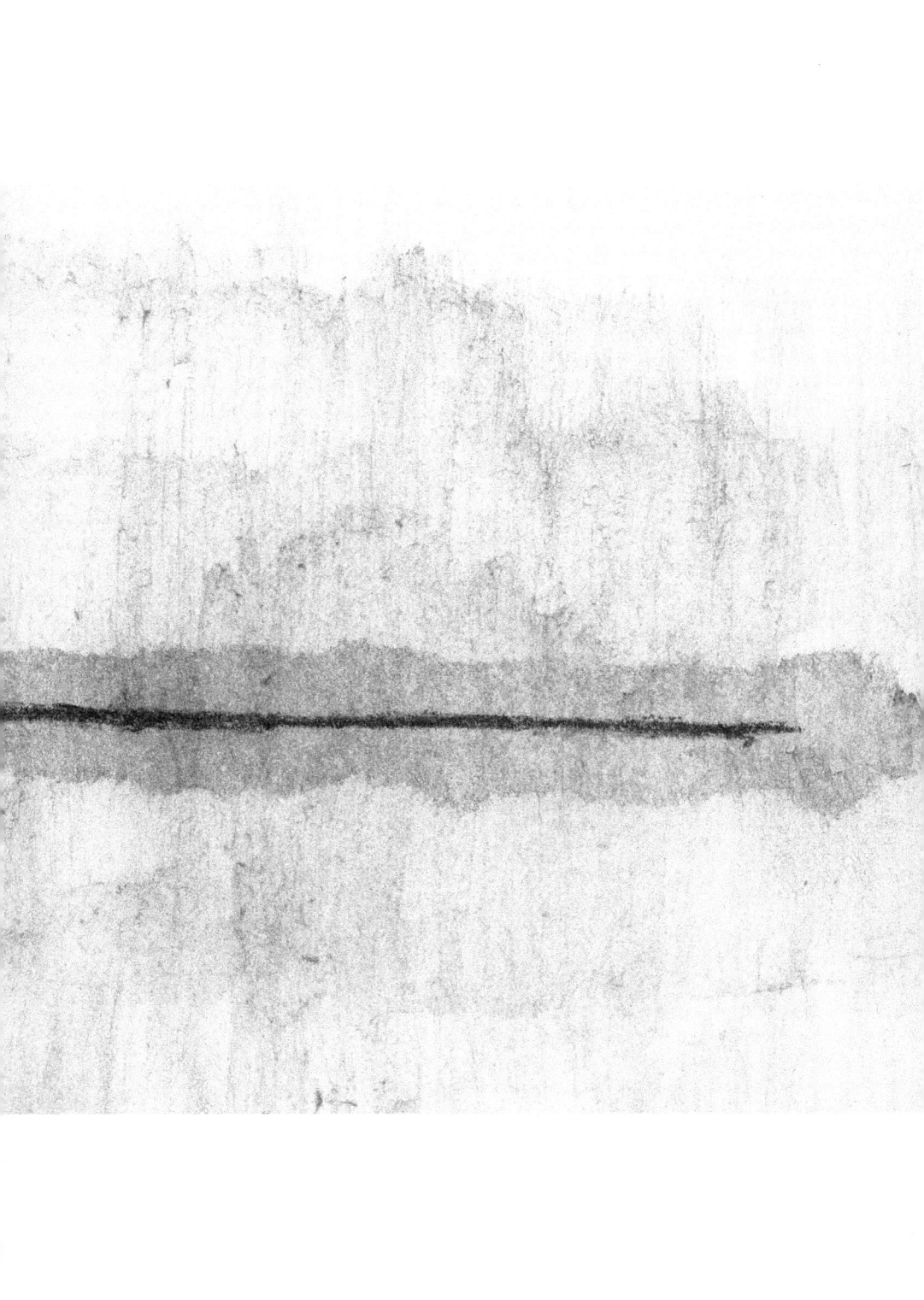

7
DISCIPLINE/
ROUTINES/
CREATIVE PRACTICES

Success is not a matter of mastering subtle, sophisticated theory but rather of embracing common sense with uncommon levels of discipline and persistence.

—Patrick Lencioni

A solid routine fosters a well-worn groove for one's mental energies and helps stave off the tyranny of moods.

—Mason Currey

We learn by practice. Whether it means to learn to dance by practicing dancing or to learn to live by practicing living, the principles are the same.

—Martha Graham

May 3, 2018

Dear Adaire,

As you have noticed within all my correspondences to date, there are many "keys" that lead to success. One of the key decisions I made to help me complete my dissertation in a timely fashion was to stop working for one year. The decision to stop working and become a full-time student was difficult because I love teaching. Ultimately, this decision ended up being the best decision I could have made because I was able to complete my dissertation and succeed in achieving my goal of earning my doctorate.

Another key decision became more important than resigning from teaching: I had to employ three indispensable attributes: discipline, routine, and creative practice. These three attributes are significant because they fueled my daily engagement with doctoral study, especially during the process of writing my dissertation. I disciplined myself with the following routines Monday through Friday.

First, I discovered the best times for both writing and reading. I found that the early morning hours are more productive for my writing, so I would write from the wee hours of the morning until the early afternoon, from 6:00 AM until 2:00–3:00 PM. In the afternoon and early evening, I found it easier to slow down and focus on reading. I would read between 2:00 and 5:00 PM. These hours were basically the same ones I kept as a teacher, so I treated my doctoral study and dissertation writing like I was going off to school to teach.

Second, I disciplined myself by engaging in routines that involved physical exercise and some creative practices to help structure my daily work schedule. For example, I would wake up around 4:30 AM to do some dancing. Dancing helped to clear my head and energize my senses. I did not just do any dancing; I was motivated by the cardio-choreography of the Fitness Marshall™ on YouTube. I watched these videos to wake up my body through dance for 20–30 minutes.

After I danced, I would take a refreshing shower and then sit down to engage in a practice created by Julia Cameron, called Morning Pages™. Essentially, Julia Cameron's concept of Morning Pages™ is a process of brain-dumping, of releasing random and cluttered thoughts in your mind through the act of longhand writing of three pages. This practice truly clears the mind and prepares an individual to focus on the task at hand, which in this context, was writing my dissertation.

After I had completed the Morning Pages™, around 6:00 AM, I would begin writing. I would write at the computer for a few hours. Between 9:00 AM and

10:00 AM every day that was not raining, I would take a break from writing and go for a walk around town or in nature. This walk would be a two-to three-mile walk that would take between 30 to 60 minutes. Walking allowed me time to process and think about the work I had been doing. Often, my thoughts became clearer and more concise, and conceptual breakthroughs occurred when I allowed myself the chance to walk, think, reflect, and breathe in the fresh air. I found that walking physically, mentally, emotionally, and spiritually aligned my being. After a good walk, I returned to the task of writing and continued my work with new insights, perspectives, and resolutions.

For a half-hour lunch around 1:30 PM, I would take a break, and often watched TV while I ate to decompress my brain from all the writing. Around 2:00 PM I would finish any writing as needed and shift into reading for the afternoon. I allowed myself the chance to digest my lunch and digest the ideas of others through reading articles or books. I would find a good spot in my home, either the couch, porch, or deck—depending upon the weather. I would read critically and make notations for my work.

Between 4:00 PM and 4:30 PM I allowed myself some time to meditate. I used meditations by Sonia Choquette or Winter Robinson to focus and center myself. Monday through Friday, between 5:00 PM and 7:00 PM, I exercised by going for a walk with my friend or by running with my running buddies, using that time to unwind and decompress from a busy workday. After a walk or run, I often engaged in painting to stimulate further my passion and process my daily work. I followed this schedule consistently during the week. I used the weekends to re-charge, create more art, and follow-up with my senior advisor and doctoral committee members.

I hope you consider trying all or some of these practices. I am very interested in hearing if and how they work for you! I also want to remind you that what I have shared regarding practices and routines is what worked for me to discipline myself to complete my dissertation. I do not necessarily think that you need to have the same amount or type of practices and routines. The important thing is that you engage creative practices and design a routine that fits your needs and/or lifestyle in order to discipline yourself to engage and complete your doctoral study and dissertation.

Creative Activity: Dancing

MORNING ROUTINE

MATERIALS
- ☐ Computer with Internet access
- ☐ YouTube Channel:
  https://www.youtube.com/user/TheFitnessMarshall/videos

ACTION STEPS

1. Browse The Fitness Marshall™ dance videos. There are a variety of artists and music genres from which to choose that Caleb Marshall, aka the Fitness Marshall™, has created.
   » I personally enjoy the following videos: Sia's "Cheap Thrills," Usher's "Yeah," Rhianna's "This Is What You Came For," and "S&M"!
2. Watch the videos and follow the Fitness Marshall's™ lead.
3. Don't worry if you are uncoordinated. This activity is about waking up your body by dancing and moving about.

Creative Activity: Morning Pages™ Julia Cameron

Julia Cameron is the author of several works that have helped artists and others connect to their creativity. *The Artist Way* is her most famous work, and the Morning Pages exercise came from this resource. It is a must read!

RESOURCE

Cameron, J. (2002/2016). *The artist's way.* New York, NY: Penguin/Putnam Inc.

LETTER 7   STRICKLAND

Creative Activity: Walking

MATERIALS

- ☐ Comfortable socks and footwear
- ☐ Fitbit™ or pedometer device (optional)

ACTION STEPS

1. Choose a couple of locations that aesthetically appeal to your senses.
   » urban, rural, woods, beach, etc.
2. Walk briskly or slowly for 20–60 minutes.
3. Breathe in the fresh air and allow your senses to be open to nature and to the environment around you.
   » Do not use sunglasses, cellphones, or iPods™/portable music players.

RESOURCE

Cameron, J. (2003). *Walking in this world.* New York, NY: Penguin/Putnam Inc.

Creative Activity: Guided Meditation

AFTERNOON ROUTINE

MATERIALS

- ☐ CD player and guided meditation CDs or portable music device with downloaded meditation files, or computer with Internet access
- ☐ Comfortable chair or couch
- ☐ Candle(s) (optional)

ACTION STEPS

1. Choose desired meditation CDs or playlist or sound files from the Internet.
2. If desired, light a candle and then sit or recline comfortably.
3. Play the CD and begin to breathe slowly and then close your eyes
4. Follow the instructions of the guided mediation for the designated time, usually 15–30 minutes.

RESOURCES

Choquette, S. (2007). *Meditations for receiving divine guidance, support, and healing.* [CD]. Carlsbad, CA: Hay House, Inc.

Choquette, S. (2012). *Grace, guidance, and gifts.* [CD]. Carlsbad, CA: Hay House, Inc.

Robinson, W. (2015). *Total relaxation with hemi-sync®.* [CD]. Lovingston, VA: Monroe Products.

CREATIVE ACTIVITY: EXERCISE

EVENING ROUTINES

MATERIALS

☐ Comfortable exercise apparel

ACTION STEPS

1. Choose desired exercise and location to workout.
   » There are many different forms of exercise that you can do: running, walking, swimming, weightlifting, bicycling, aerobics, etc.
2. Engage in exercise/workout for 45–60 minutes.

TIP: You may choose to exercise alone or with others. (I have found it more enjoyable and motivating to spend time and walk with my friend or run with my running buddies! Exercising with them really helps balance the time I am unable to participate in other activities due to the boundaries set for doctoral work.)

Creative Activity: Engaging Your Creativity/Passion

MATERIALS
- ☐ Desired supplies and tools for personal creative expression

ACTION STEPS
1. Choose desired creative activity. (For me, I would paint using my watercolors!)
2. Engage desired activity before and/or after you eat dinner.

TIP: The amount of time that you engage in your creativity/passion daily will depend upon your availability and the time you choose to invest. It can and most likely will vary depending upon circumstances and life events. Whether you engage for 10 minutes or for one to two hours does not matter; the most important thing is that you intentionally engage in your passion and creative expression. It is also important to be tender with yourself, and if you are unable to engage in your passion on a given day, that is also okay, as long as you are aware and mindful of expressing your creativity and feeding your passion regularly!

8
WRITING

Seeking clarity and authenticity in the face of thoughtfulness.
—Maxine Greene

Take advantage of every opportunity to practice your communication skills so that when important occasions arise, you will have the gift, the style, the sharpness, the clarity, and the emotions to affect other people.
—Jim Rohn

I know you've heard it a thousand times before. But it's true—hard work pays off. If you want to be good, you have to practice, practice, practice. If you don't love something, then don't do it.
—Ray Bradbury

May 8, 2018

Dear Adaire,

    I am glad to hear that you have begun to create some routines and engage in creative practices. I cannot emphasize enough how valuable these will be for balancing your doctoral journey. One of the most challenging yet rewarding aspects of doctoral work is the process of writing your dissertation and developing your academic voice.

    I mentioned in a previous letter that one of the struggles I experienced with doctoral study was learning to write like a scholar. Prior to doctoral study and graduate work, my experiences with writing were mostly creative in nature, such as poetry, song lyrics, and stories. At the beginning of my doctoral program, a professor explained to me that scholarly writing is structurally demanding and not the same as creative writing.

    I have come to understand that scholarly writing and academic voice is a unique style known for clarity and conciseness of thoughts and words. Developing your academic voice and scholarly writing is a time-consuming process that requires practice and perseverance. In order to be an effective writer and clearer thinker, you must put the time into developing your communication skills.

    I believe that you should write when you feel you are most open. For me, as I mentioned, I found it easier to write in the quiet of the early morning hours, so I would plan to start working between 5:00 and 6:00 AM and write until lunch time. I always felt much more energized in the morning to write, rather than in the afternoon or evening. You will need to discover the time of day or night that is most accessible for both your mind and heart to write.

    As you write, carefully work without judgment or expectation—but do write with intention. For example, begin by outlining each chapter of your dissertation and fill in the content and context as you go along. Try starting from the end and work your way backward. I found this strategy to be especially helpful once I understood the significance of my sociocultural perspective.

    Writing, like painting, requires persistence and the need to work, especially when you do not always feel like it. Once you have found your preferred time of day or night to write, you must commit and discipline yourself to work consistently. The ability to approach the page or computer screen and write when you are not necessarily inspired offers an interesting reward for showing up.

    Once you start, you will inevitably find that before you know it, you begin to experience what Mihaly Csikszentmihalyi (1990/2008) referred to as "flow," as the work seemingly emanates from the simple act of engaging writing. The more you write, the clearer your thinking becomes as your thoughts connect easily. The clearer your thinking becomes, the easier it becomes to write simply. The ability to write and express with clarity and simplicity is essential for communicating the most basic and the most sophisticated ideas. Developing your academic voice and capacity to articulate through writing is one of the significant hallmarks of doctoral scholarship.

RESOURCES

Csikszentmihalyi, M. (1990/2008). *Flow: The psychology of optimal experience.* New York, NY: HarperCollins Publishers.

Graff, G., & Birkenstein, C. (2014). *They say, I say: The moves that matter in academic writing.* New York NY: W. W. Norton and Company, Inc.

Williams, J., & Bizup, J. (2016). *Style: Lessons in clarity and grace.* London, UK: Pearson.

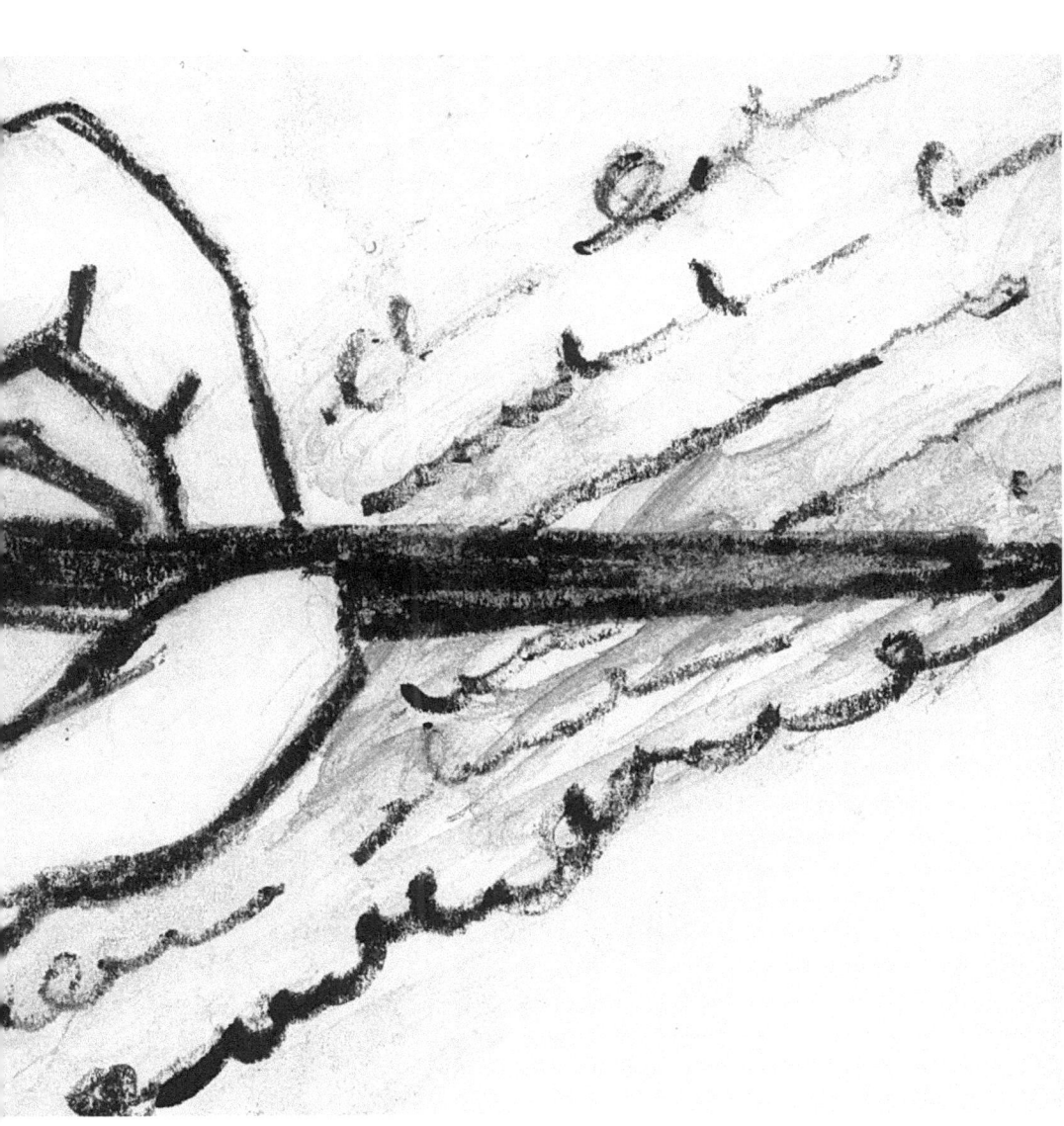

9 READING

Reading is to the mind what exercise is to the body.
—Joseph Addison

When you read about the lives of other people, people of different circumstances or similar circumstances, you are part of their lives for that moment. You inhabit their lives, and you feel what they're feeling, and that is compassion. If we see that reading does allow us that, we see how absolutely essential reading is.
—Amy Tan

May 12, 2018

Dear Adaire,

I trust you are familiar with the phrase, "Reading is fundamental." This phrase is not only a slogan to promote children's literacy but also a great cultural truth. If you want to be successful at writing and communicating, and being a doctoral scholar, then you have to be literate and you must read.

Similar to my advice on writing in my previous letter, you must discover when you are open to reading and then read a lot! I cannot overemphasize this point enough: *Read. Read. Read!*

Read articles, books, magazines, newspapers, journals, and blogs. I discovered my love for reading when I realized what I was truly passionate about. It is no surprise that the books I read center around my interests in the arts, creativity, and spirituality, as well as teaching and learning. I have delighted in reading a variety of authors and topics over the years and find it most exciting when I discover convergent threads between differing authors and ideas.

Reading is important for both developing the mind and functioning in society. It is used to educate, influence, and expand perspectives. Reading can also strengthen an individual's imagination, creativity, and self-expression. I have heard that reading is also at the heart of a democratic society. I could go on about the importance of reading, and there are many dissertations about the significance of reading, literature, and literacy. However, all I really want to do is impress upon you that reading is essential to your doctoral study, research, and dissertation—even and especially works that you may not think are directly connected (or connected at all) to your doctoral work.

Doctoral study heavily involves reading and exploring others' ideas, beliefs, and philosophies. When you are engaging in your dissertation literature review, read interdisciplinary works from other content areas to help create a more holistic perspective and understanding of your area of focus. Look for the connections to inspire your imagination and thinking process.

I found that reading in the afternoon or in the evening just before bed gave me great fodder for my nightly dreams and processing. I created a cyclical balance between writing in the morning and reading in the afternoons, which helped me with developing my dissertation writing. Perhaps you would want to consider creating such a balance between your writing routine and reading practice. Good luck and don't forget to *Read. Read. Read!*

RESOURCES

Berger, W. (2014). *A more beautiful question.* New York, NY: Bloomsbury.

Dweck, C. (2006). *Mindset.* New York, NY: Ballantine Books.

Gardner, H. (2006). *Multiple intelligences: New horizons in theory and practice.* New York, NY: Basic Books.

Herman, A. (2016). *Visual intelligence.* New York, NY: Houghton Mifflin Harcourt.

Langer, E. J. (1997). *The power of mindful learning.* Cambridge, MA: Da Capo Press/Perseus Books.

Martin, R. (2009). *The opposable mind.* Boston, MA: Harvard Business Press.

Pink, D. (2006). *A whole new mind.* New York, NY: Riverhead Books.

Robinson, K. (2001). *Out of our minds: Learning to be creative.* West Sussex, UK: Capstone Publishing Ltd.

Schön, D. A. (1983). *The reflective practitioner: How professionals think in action.* U.S.A.: Basic Books, Inc.

Takacs, D. (2003, Summer). How does your positionality bias your epistemology? *Thought and Action: NEA Higher Education Journal, 27*-38

Thomas, D., & Brown, J. S. (2011). *A new culture of learning: Cultivating the imagination for a world of constant change.* Lexington, KY: CreateSpace.

10
CLEANING AND ORGANIZING

Cleanliness is a state of purity, clarity, and precision.
—Suze Orman

When your environment is clean, you feel happy, motivated, and healthy.
—Lailah Gifty Akita

Cleaning and organizing is a practice, not a project.
—Meagan Francis

May 15, 2018

Dear Adaire,

In this correspondence, I want to address how cleaning and organizing can be cathartic for you and your doctoral study. In order for me to feel less distracted, I need to be organized and have clean spaces around me. Thus, one of the "tricks" I used to keep me on track with doctoral study was to clean and organize periodically in order to avoid feeling distracted by trying to keep up with too many details.

Cleaning periodically eliminates the nagging voice inside that tries to sidetrack you from staying focused on your work. Taking preemptive measures and cleaning periodically allows your mental self the space to stay focused. This kind of "mental cleansing" is very similar to the work that your mind does for you when you meditate.

In addition to the routines that you create, you should also consider creating deadlines as a way to organize and help create a sense of urgency for yourself with your work. Organizing your schedule with timeframes can be helpful as it inspires action. Furthermore, being organized is a critical part of honoring the boundaries you have created to allow yourself to engage in doctoral study.

I assume you are wondering how cleaning a space or organizing your time produces clarity and insight for doctoral work. You might find it interesting that research actually documents the psychological effects of clutter (McMains & Kastner, 2011; Ryback, 2016; Whitbourne, 2017). Psychologically, clutter makes it difficult to focus on a particular task. According to Dr. Ralph Ryback, "The visual cortex becomes overwhelmed by task-irrelevant objects, which makes it harder to allocate attention and complete tasks efficiently."

Essentially, cleaning helps to make mental space and room for ideas to flow without distractions; moreover, organization is key to moving forward and completing work tasks efficiently. Even now that my doctoral study is over, whenever I get stuck in my process or feel distracted, whether it is with a writing project or even painting, I make sure that I clean my work desk or art studio and organize my responsibilities. Cleaning and organizing mentally shifts me into a place where I can focus and return to the task at hand.

One of the things that helps to make the task of cleaning and organizing enjoyable is listening to music. Two musical groups always accompany my cleaning efforts, and these are the Supremes and Fleetwood Mac. The songs performed by both groups are easy listening and symbolically perfect for the process of purging and cleansing.

Next time you feel stuck or distracted, take a little bit of time to clean some space and organize your responsibilities. This process will help you to experience a shift, allowing you to realign your focus on the doctoral work and task before you. You will discover that the mere act of cleaning, both metaphorically and literally, presents a sense of accomplishment. When you clean, you unclutter your virtual and tangible spaces. When you are organized, it gives you a peaceful sense that feels good and gives you room to breathe and work. I have provided the names of a few soundtracks that I have found to be wonderful to listen to when cleaning and organizing. I encourage you to try my recommendations, or even better, discover your own soundtracks that would make cleaning an enjoyable and cathartic experience for you.

RESOURCES

Diana Ross + The Supremes. (1997). *The ultimate collection* [CD]. New York, NY: Motown Records/Universal Music Group.

Fleetwood Mac. (1988). *Greatest hits* [CD]. Burbank, CA: Warner Bros. Records.

11
OPENNESS TO FEEDBACK

In order for people to make progress, they have to get feedback and information on how they're doing.

—Daniel Pink

Be thoughtful about what you need and what you're being offered, and get aligned.

—Douglas Stone & Sheila Heen

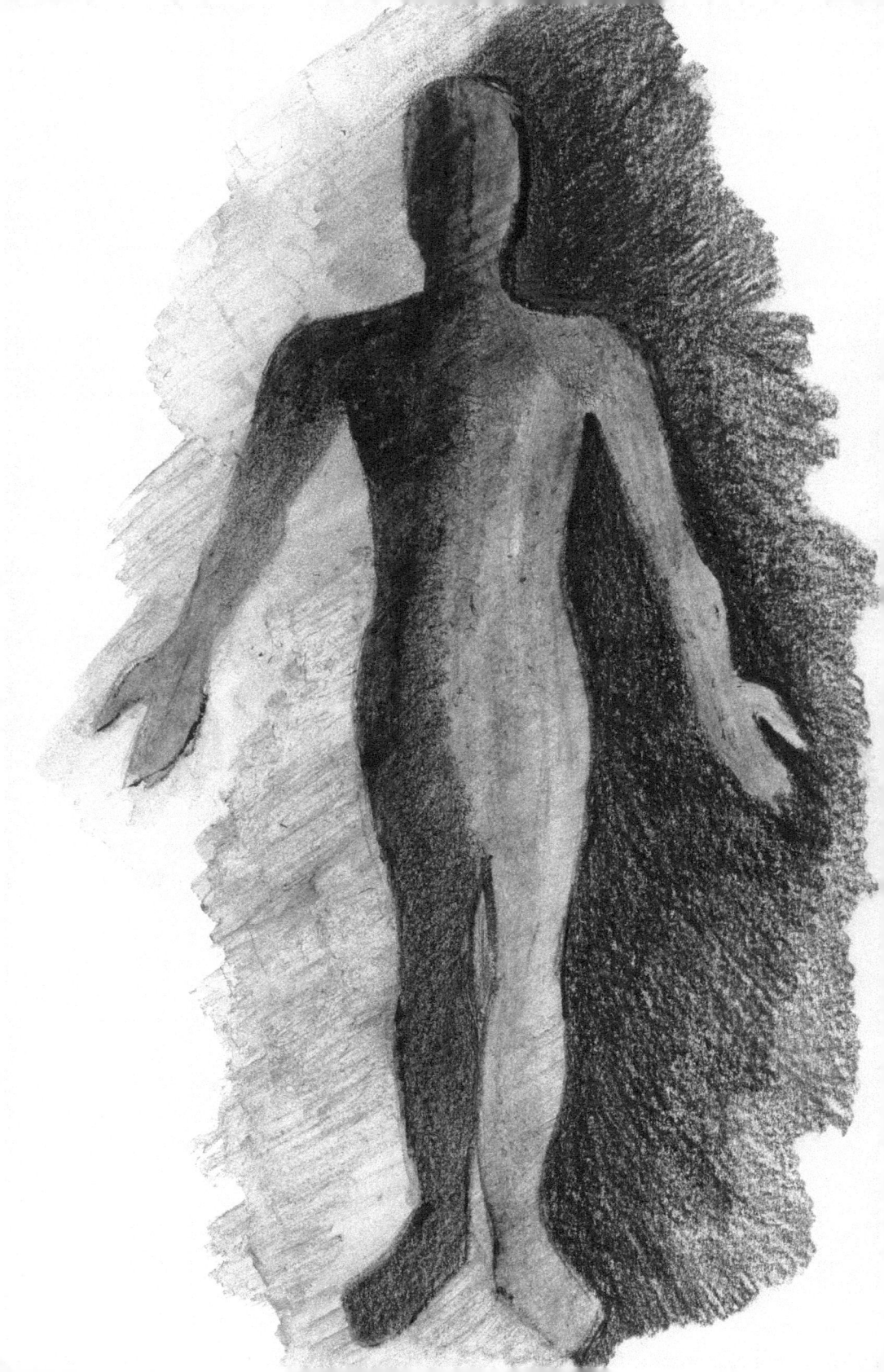

May 17, 2018

Dear Adaire,

One of the most important pieces of advice I can offer you, based on my personal experience, is to be open to feedback. Being open to the feedback from my professors, senior advisor, and doctoral committee members was instrumental in helping me grow as a scholar and complete my dissertation. During the course of my doctoral study, I observed peers in my doctoral program who resisted this process, unable to accept some of the feedback given to them from the professors or doctoral committee. Sadly, their lack of openness to receiving and integrating feedback into their learning created a lot of frustration and stagnation in their doctoral process. For example, one colleague did not follow the directions for a specific protocol involving qualitative research methods, which resulted in multiple revisions of an assignment before it was deemed complete.

Another example that involves feedback is the importance of identifying an issue or problem to address and knowing what you want to learn from it. Colleagues that did not synthesize the critical feedback they received into a clear problem statement to guide their inquiry experienced impasses that prevented them from efficiently moving into their research and dissertation phase. This resulted in individuals feeling emotionally and intellectually bereft toward the process, and toward constructive criticism.

Knowledge can be empowering. To understand the value of feedback, it is imperative to understand constructive criticism. According to Douglas Stone and Sheila Heen, authors of the book, *Thanks for the Feedback*, feedback is the information and constructive criticism we get about ourselves. We receive and need three primary forms of feedback:

» Appreciation
» Coaching
» Evaluation

As you embark on your doctoral journey, you must remember that your senior advisor and doctoral committee members are experienced and therefore can help you navigate the doctoral process.

Being open to the feedback the doctoral committee gives you regarding your research plan and dissertation writing is so important. It is human nature to be stubborn and think our own perspective is the only "right" one. We often think that we do not need or want to receive any advice that is presented to us.

However, in the context of doctoral study, the advice, suggestions, and feedback provided by your senior advisor and doctoral committee is intended to stretch and strengthen your thinking, as well as enhance the clarity of your academic voice. Doctoral candidates who are open and receptive to feedback reflect upon the information provided and learn to integrate it into their work. Resistance to feedback creates unnecessary frustration and stagnation, and impedes the doctoral journey.

Having boundaries and humility is crucial for being open to receiving feedback. These two attributes are important for the following reasons. As I explained early on, exercising boundaries allows you to advocate for yourself and your needs, which essentially drives your own learning. Earlier I explained boundaries in the context of your personal life. Now this lesson informs how you engage with your academic relationships.

Learning to ask for the type of feedback you need is vital to your personal growth. Likewise, having the ability to turn down or turn away unwanted feedback is critical for lifelong learning. When you can articulate your needs, you will end up receiving clearer information from those offering their advice.

Bottom line, feedback is essential if you want to learn and grow. Exercising humility allows you to appreciate truly the wisdom and experience individuals possess and are willing to share with you. Humility fosters gratitude and an awareness of the influence of others and their contributions for your personal success. This awareness was especially true for me, within the context of being guided through my doctoral journey by my senior advisor and doctoral committee.

The ultimate goal is to be able to integrate feedback into your work. To help you, I provide instructions at the end of this letter for a three-step practice to align explicitly the purpose of what you need and what you're receiving for feedback. These steps may be an unfamiliar and even uncomfortable process at first. However, I assure you that once you are able to understand and engage feedback, then you will be better equipped to learn, grow, and succeed, especially as it pertains to the process of doctoral study. Exercise this practice the next time you receive feedback from someone and please let me know what you think!

RESOURCES

Goleman, D. (1995/2005). *Emotional intelligence.* New York, NY: Bantam Books.

Goleman, D. (2007). *Social intelligence.* New York, NY: Bantam Books.

Kegan, R., & Lahey, L. L. (2001). *How the way we talk can change the way we work*. San Francisco, CA: Jossey-Bass.

Pink, D. (2009). *Drive*. New York, NY: Riverhead Books.

Stone, D., & Heen, S. (2014). *Thanks for the feedback*. New York, NY: Penguin Books.

CREATIVE ACTIVITY: FEEDBACK PRACTICE: LISTEN, REVIEW, ASK

Inspired by the work of Douglas Stone & Sheila Heen.

MATERIALS

1. *Listen.* When you engage someone, who is giving you feedback, listen carefully to what is presented and how it is being delivered.

2. *Review.* Identify what type of feedback you are receiving and how it connects to the purpose of your meeting or the topic of discussion. Feedback usually falls into these three categories:
   » Appreciation
   » Coaching
   » Evaluation

3. *Ask.* After reviewing the feedback, ask yourself if the feedback provided is useful for you. After determining the relevancy of the feedback or if you are not sure about the feedback, ask for the provider's intention and the reasons for providing this type of feedback. Furthermore, if the feedback is not necessarily helpful or clear, ask the provider for the type of feedback you need and would like, given the context.

12
WAITING AND WALKING WITH HUMILITY

Humility is the solid foundation of all virtues.

—Confucius

What humility does for one is it reminds us that there are people before me. I have already been paid for.

And what I need to do is prepare myself so that I can pay for someone else who has yet to come but who may be here and needs me.

—Maya Angelou

May 21, 2018

Dear Adaire,

 I was reading your last correspondence and I detected a sense of urgency in your message. When coming to a crossroads within the doctoral process, it can be difficult to be patient or accept the advice or perspective of others. Your sense of impatience reminded of a saying my senior advisor, Dr. Francine Jennings, shared with me: "You need to wait with humility." As you are undoubtedly starting to realize, doctoral study and the doctoral process are truly an ebb and flow experience. Many times, you will be moving swiftly and then experience a stall or sudden halt. To make a music analogy, if you will, a pause occurs in the playing of your soundtrack. For example, you can have your dissertation and research proposal approved by your doctoral committee, but then the proposal must be reviewed by your institution's Internal Review Board (IRB) to make sure that you have accounted for the safety and well-being of the participants you wish to work with in your research.

 The IRB review process takes several weeks, even months, and the waiting can feel unbearable. A dear friend of mine had this very experience. After waiting two months for her doctoral committee's approval, she was finally able to submit her dissertation proposal to IRB. Once submitted to IRB, my friend had to wait another two months until IRB approved her dissertation proposal.

 One of the primary reasons my friend's IRB approval took so long was that she wanted to conduct research with youth. IRB's scrutiny of a dissertation proposal, or any research proposal, is severely scrupulous, especially when research involves the safety and well-being of children.

 IRB has an ethical and legal obligation to support the welfare of human subjects who participate in research. I am happy to note that despite the long wait my friend endured, it was worth it as she is passionately engaged in her research. She has come to realize the truth in Theodore Roosevelt's words, "Nothing worth having was ever achieved without effort."

 Another example requiring humility is when you complete a chapter of your dissertation and then you must wait for feedback from your doctoral committee members. Waiting for someone else to do their part, such as reviewing your research plan or editing your chapter, can be difficult and feel excruciating. In these moments, you must exercise patience and wait with humility.

 Waiting like this means that you breathe through the tension of uncertainty and trust that others are doing their best for your best. We are quite presumptuous to think that we know everything, especially regarding doctoral study, which is a new experience for you. The doctoral process is designed as a space to help us learn and grow through the wisdom and experience of others, such as the IRB or your doctoral committee members.

Waiting with humility releases assumptions to allow the necessary process to unfold, or as Shaun McNiff likes to say, allow us to "trust the process" of your experience. Essentially, I am trying to convey to you that doctoral scholarship and the doctoral process has a long history. Doctoral scholarship has its roots in the European Middle Ages, as well as the 19th Century United States. The doctoral process has been around long before you or I were ever born, so its ebb and flow nature have profound merit.

I am sure you're questioning the relevancy of all this information, wondering how this is supposed to help your current feelings and state of mind. Following are two activities that I do to help me remember to wait with humility. The first activity is a breathing meditation. The simple act of breathing physically distracts the focus of "waiting" and clears the mind, while energizing the body with essential oxygen. Breathing can also be a form of meditation, as you are focusing on the locus of your control. You will learn that there are limitations that we control very little as individuals in life. Discovering the locus of what is in your control is part of this kind of waiting. Breathing is within the locus of your control and you can learn to breathe to help you exercise patience so you can wait successfully with humility.

The second activity is walking with humility. For me, this means exercising with a very specific intention. In this case, it is a combination of the breathing exercise previously described and a walk. Both of these activities were inspired by meditative practices presented by Sonia Choquette in her book, *Your 3 Best Super Powers*. I have shared this resource and directions for these activities to help you. When you are feeling anxious or need a reminder to wait with humility, try either of these activities—I guarantee these will help calm your nerves and mind!

RESOURCE

Choquette, S. (2016). *Your 3 best super powers*. Carlsbad, CA: Hay House, Inc.

Creative Activity: Waiting with Humility (Breathing Meditation)

MATERIALS

☐ Comfortable chair

ACTION STEPS

1. Whenever you feel the tension in your body or mental stress, allow yourself to pause and take a minute or two to breathe and recenter.
2. Take a seat and close your eyes.
3. Feel the tension and stress as you slowly inhale through your nose.
4. Hold the breath for three seconds.
5. Feel the tension and stress release as you slowly exhale the breath through your mouth.
6. Repeat this process a few times.
7. Open your eyes and slowly stand up and return to what you were doing with a recharged spirit.

Creative Activity: Walking with Humility (Walking Meditation)

MATERIALS

☐ Comfortable socks and footwear

ACTION STEPS

Take a 20-minute walk and follow this four-step process:

1. Breathe in through your nose for a count of four.
2. Hold the breath for a count of four.

3. Exhale the breath through your mouth for a count of four.
4. Count to four after all the air is released and then repeat.

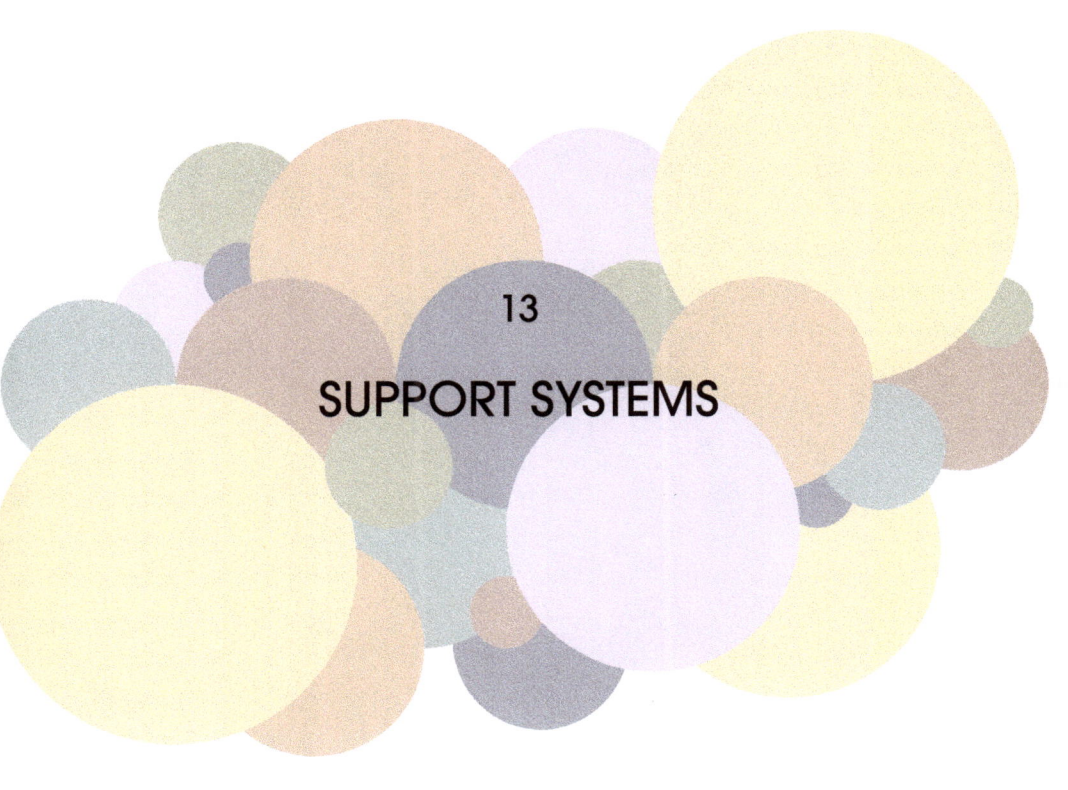

13
SUPPORT SYSTEMS

What you seek is seeking you.

—Rumi

Every successful individual knows that his or her achievement depends on a community of persons working together.

—Paul Ryan

Choose to focus your time, energy and conversation around people who inspire you, support you and help you to grow you into your happiest, strongest, wisest self.

—Karen Salmansohn

May 27, 2018

Dear Adaire,

 I have been thinking about our recent exchanges and I would be remiss if I did not comment on the necessity of support systems. Support systems can be a blessing for motivating personal growth and achievement. Although it is important that you have the support from friends and family, I am specifically referring to a support system that is educationally based and understands the experiences with doctoral study.

 As Dewey (1938) espoused, learning is a social experience, and being able to share and work through ideas and assignments with others deepens the educative experience. Working together is an invaluable concept that cannot be underestimated. One of the primary reasons I have been successful in completing my dissertation and earning my doctorate degree in a timely fashion is the fact that I had a great support system and learning community through the cohort model established by Lesley University. If you are not familiar with it, a cohort is a group of adult students working together through an educational curriculum or program. The cohort model for graduate-level learning is powerful because it is a small, student-centered, nurturing learning community that is non-competitive and provides professional networking opportunities.

 My cohort experience provided amazing support, care, understanding, and accountability to one another, as well as the doctoral learning process. I am aware that not all universities have cohort models, which makes me a little sad. I cannot begin to imagine how I could have done my doctoral scholarship without the vital support and help of others who traveled this road alongside me.

 If your doctoral program does not have a designated cohort model, then I would recommend creating a support system and little learning community of your own. If you inquire through social media or your institution's student activity center, you will find that people crave connection and community.

 Your support system or learning community does not need to be large; two or three people would be perfect. By surrounding yourself with people who support and understand the doctoral challenges and process, you will develop a deep camaraderie that will provide both the academic and logistical support necessary to engage doctoral scholarship and complete your doctoral program requirements.

RESOURCES

Brown, B. (2012). *Daring greatly.* New York, NY: Gotham Books.

Cameron, J. (2006). *Finding water.* New York, NY: Tarcher.

Hooks, B. (2003). *Teaching community.* New York, NY: Routledge.

Palmer, P. (1990). *The active life.* San Francisco, CA: Jossey-Bass.

14
GRATITUDE

Gratitude makes sense of our past, brings peace for today, and creates a vision for tomorrow.

—Melody Beattie

Gratitude is essential to happiness.

—Marianne Williamson

The discipline of gratitude is the explicit effort to acknowledge that all I am and have is given to me as a gift of love, a gift to be celebrated with joy.

—Henri Nouwen

As we express our gratitude, we must never forget that the highest appreciation is not to utter words, but to live by them.

—John F. Kennedy

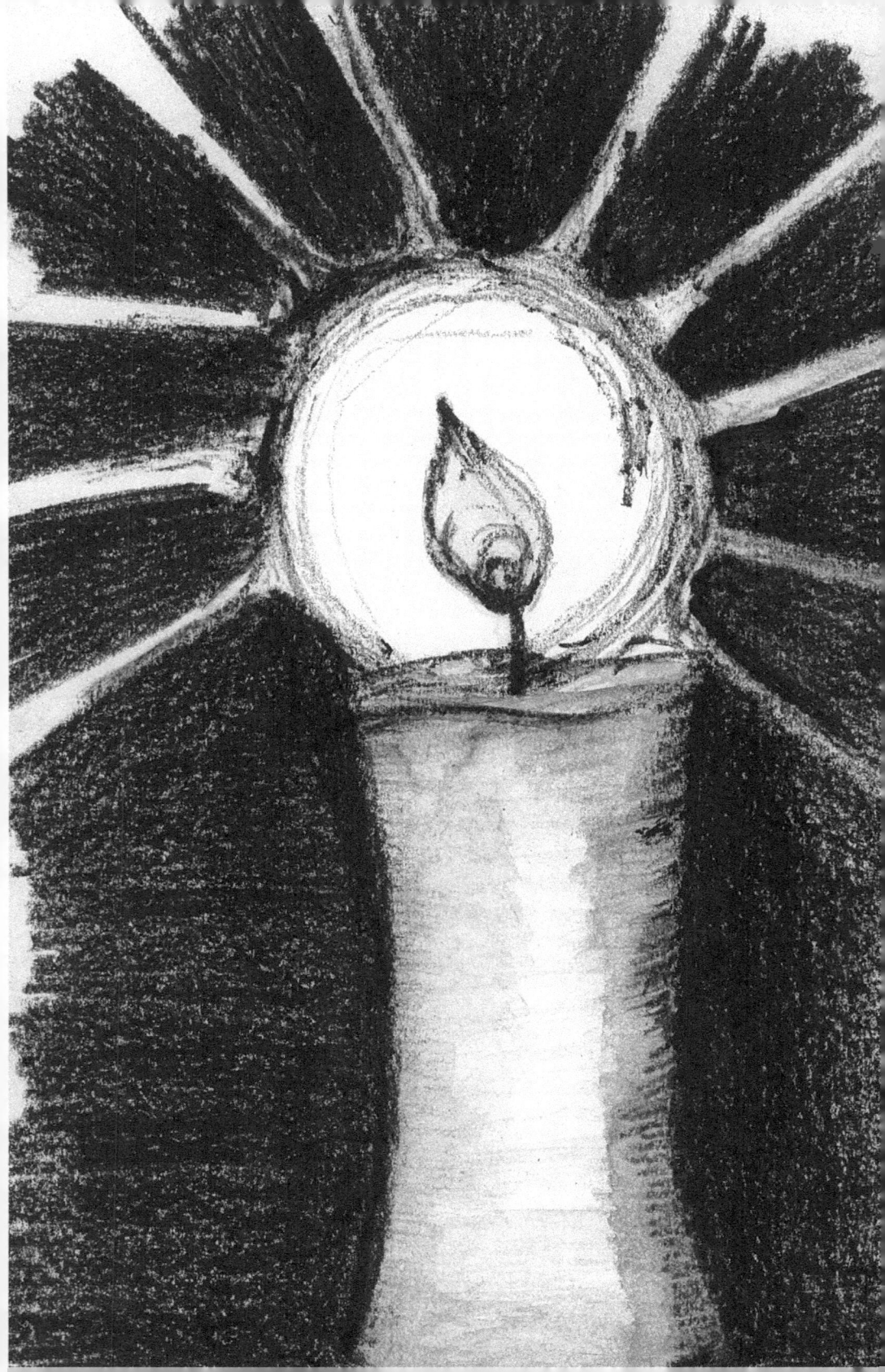

June 2, 2018

Dear Adaire,

I am thrilled to hear that you continue to experiment and explore some of the routines and creative practices I have shared. It is exciting to learn that the way you are disciplining yourself to engage doctoral scholarship is working. Keeping this in mind, one of the final "secrets" to my success with doctoral scholarship that I will share with you is also a key ingredient to life in general. This key ingredient is gratitude.

Gratitude is a universal expression and is defined by Angeles Arrien (2013) as, "the recognition of the unearned increments of value in one's experience." Gratitude reminds us of what matters most in our life and can transform it by inviting a profound spiritual influence that affects our holistic beings. Gratitude is both a mindset and an endeavor. As a mindset, gratitude is the attitude and disposition that focuses on thankfulness, appreciation, and generosity. As an endeavor, gratitude is a dynamic practice of reflection, awareness, and expression.

Integrating gratitude into your doctoral study and life will open yourself up to new insights and wisdom that will ultimately enhance your inherent nature, as well as doctoral scholarship. Gratitude is so important because, as Melody Beattie eloquently stated,

> *Gratitude unlocks the fullness of life. It turns what we have into enough, and more. It turns denial into acceptance, chaos to order, confusion to clarity. It can turn a meal into a feast, a house into a home, a stranger into a friend.*

You will discover there is much to be grateful for along the journey of doctoral scholarship. Examples of gratitude that I have include developing my academic voice and having the ability to turn a phrase with clarity and grace, engaging in purposeful research and making scholarly contributions to the world, and the interpersonal relationships and connections I have cultivated through my doctoral program.

All of these examples are invaluable hallmarks of doctoral scholarship that truly incur gratitude. With each step of the doctoral process, it is important that you are open to expanding your awareness of the abundant blessings and learning experiences that distinguish your path along your doctoral journey.

I am sure you're wondering exactly how I made gratitude a daily practice. I have found the following practices to be most helpful in integrating gratitude into my daily life. First, I made it a point to journal and write down my gratitude. Second, I got into the habit of speaking gratitude out loud, literally saying "Thanks" or "Thank you, God" and naming precisely what it is for which I am thankful. (I would speak gratitude aloud, of course, in the privacy of my home or car.) Third, I engaged in prayer and gratitude meditations. Part of this practice involved exchanging daily affirmations and messages with a friend via texting to motivate and inspire gratitude. Finally, another friend of mine introduced me to the concept of a gratitude jar. This concept is the physical act of writing your gratitude and placing it in a jar to collect your gratitude experiences. The gratitude jar is a wonderful and visible reminder of the milestones you have achieved.

I placed notes in my gratitude jar to signify events or experiences, such as completing my qualifying paper, submitting my dissertation proposal, receiving IRB approval to conduct my qualitative research, completing the data collection and analysis phases of my research process, and, of course, successfully defending my dissertation, as well as receiving my formal commencement notice.

Reviewing the contents of the jar once in a while can remind you of the gifts, blessings, and reasons for your gratitude. You must remember to give thanks, as well as express gratitude wholeheartedly and with authenticity. Being grateful and expressing it can be difficult at times, especially when you are stressed, overwhelmed, and experiencing setbacks.

During these types of moments, I turned to nature, creativity, and others for perspective, as well as renewed connection. Allowing nature's beauty and mystery to fill your senses can instill gratitude. Walking the beach always fills me with gratitude. Engaging my creativity, such as painting or artmaking, was also a sure way to invoke gratitude. Offering connection and gratitude to others through notes, letters, texts, emails, and phone calls can reciprocally fill you with gratitude.

I have provided some literary resources to help you further explore and appreciate the power of gratitude. I have also provided directions for some of the creative activities and gratitude practices I mentioned. There are so many different ways you can integrate gratitude into doctoral study, as well as your overall life. I look forward to hearing about how you engage gratitude and the practices you use. Sadly, I also realize that this is my last letter to you. In a poetic sense, our correspondence ends right where it began—with gratitude.

Thank you for giving me the opportunity to share my insights and experience of doctoral scholarship with you. I hope you have found my letters to be helpful and beneficial to your doctoral journey. I know you will do an amazing job with your doctoral study. I eagerly look forward to celebrating your completed dissertation and doctoral achievement. Until then, with an open mind and grateful heart, onwards and upwards ...

RESOURCES

Arrien, A. (2013). *Living in gratitude.* Boulder, CO: Sounds True, Inc.

Beattie, M. (2007). *Gratitude.* Center City, MN: Hazeldon.

Cameron, J. (1997). *Heart steps.* New York, NY: Tarcher.

Cameron, J. (1998). *Blessings.* New York, NY: Tarcher.

Cameron, J. (2016). *Life lessons.* New York, NY: Tarcher.

Ehrmann, M. (1927/1995). *Desiderata.* New York, NY: Crown Publishers, Inc.

CREATIVE ACTIVITY: GRATITUDE JOURNAL

MATERIALS
- ☐ Notebook/Journal
- ☐ Computer
- ☐ Pen/Pencil

ACTION STEPS
1. Document your gratitude by writing it down in a journal or notebook, or by creating a file on a computer.
2. Make sure to date your entries and be as specific as possible with the details of your gratitude.
3. Repeat this process whenever you are moved or filled with gratitude.

Creative Activity: Gratitude Jar

MATERIALS

- ☐ Pieces of paper
- ☐ Pen/Pencil
- ☐ Mason jar (small or large)

ACTION STEPS

1. Find a Mason jar (small or large) and label it with the word "Gratitude" or the current date, including the year.

2. On a piece of paper, write down the gratitude you have for any event, milestone, or accomplishment you experience along the journey of your doctoral study. (Make sure to be specific with details of the experience and the date!)

3. Fill the jar accordingly and consistently.

4. Occasionally review the contents of the jar to remind yourself of the gratitude you have experienced. (This review can be especially helpful during times of stress or if you experience any setbacks.)

EPILOGUE

The real gift of gratitude is that the more grateful you are, the more present you become.

—Robert Holden

Adaire graduated and made plans to move out west for a period of time to explore, grow, and prepare to enter graduate school. Before she left, she sent me the following letter:

Dear Strickland ... um, Christopher,
My relationship and journey with you have been one of the most meaningful experiences in this life, and even though I'm moving away for a time, I will stay in touch and keep you in my mind and heart. You are an incredible teacher, and I'm so grateful and appreciative to have had your influence in my growth, both as a person and as an artist. Cheers to the best photography teacher I've ever had, and one of the kindest, most authentic souls I'll ever know.
Best,
Adaire
P.S. It's gonna take me some time to get used to not calling you Strickland.

When I receive a message like Adaire's, I find myself awed, humbled, and full of gratitude. I cannot think of any other profession or way I would want to focus my energy than through teaching and learning with others. Teaching is fundamentally about relationships.

I have been blessed to have made some wonderful connections and fortunate to have cultivated some amazing relationships along this journey of life. Now that I have earned my doctorate, I look forward to a new phase in my professional career as I pursue teaching in and through the arts in higher education.

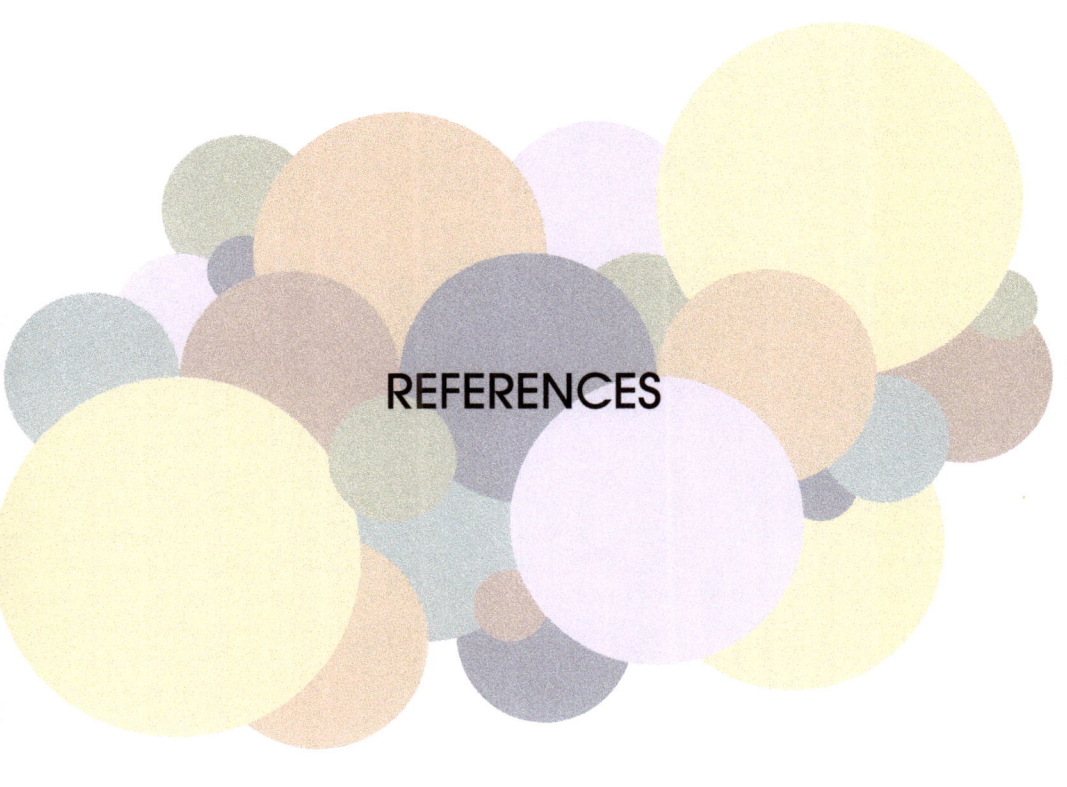

REFERENCES

Adams, T., Holman Jones, S. & Ellis, C. (2015). *Autoethnography: Understanding qualitative research.* New York, NY: Oxford University Press.

Arrien, A. (2013). *Living in gratitude.* Boulder, CO: Sounds True, Inc.

Brown, B. (2010). *The gifts of imperfection.* Center City, MN: Hazelden.

Brown, B. (2015). *Rising strong: The reckoning, the rumble, the revolution.* New York, NY: Spiegel & Grau.

Cameron, J. (2002/2016). *The Artist Way.* New York, NY: Penguin/Putnam Inc.

Cary, J. (2017). *How architecture can create dignity for all.* [Video File]. Retrieved from *https://www.ted.com/talks/john_cary_how_architecture_can_create_dignity_for_ all*

Csikszentmihalyi, M. (1990/2008). *Flow: The psychology of optimal experience.* New York, NY: HarperCollins Publishers.

Dewey, J. (1938). *Experience and education.* New York, NY: Touchstone.

McMains, S., & Kastner, S. (2011). Interactions of top-down and bottom-up mechanisms in human visual cortex. *Journal of Neuroscience*, 31(2), 587-97.

McNiff, S. (1998). *Trust the process.* Boston, MA: Shambhala Publications, Inc.

Palmer, P. (1983/1993). *To know as we are known: Education as a spiritual practice.* New York, NY: HarperOne.

Robinson, K. (2009). *The element.* New York, NY: The Penguin Group.

Ryback, R. (2016). *The powerful psychology behind cleanliness: How to stay organized—and reap the health benefits.* Retrieved from *https://www.psychologytoday. com/us/blog/the-truisms-wellness/201607/the-powerful-psychology-behind-cleanliness*

Stone, D., & Heen, S. (2014). *Thanks for the feedback.* New York, NY: Penguin Books.

Whitbourne, S.K. (2017). *5 reasons to clear the clutter out of your life: New research shows why it's better to live a cleaner and less cluttered life.* Retrieved from *https:// www.psychologytoday.com/us/blog/fulfillment-any-age/201705/5-reasons-clear-the-clutter-out-your-life*

www.ingramcontent.com/pod-product-compliance
Lightning Source LLC
Chambersburg PA
CBHW041128110526
44592CB00020B/2721